THE GREAT CHICAGO FIRE

All Is Not Lost

BY STEVEN OTFINOSKI

Consultant:
Richard Bell, PhD
Associate Professor of History
University of Maryland, College Park

CAPSTONE PRESS
a capstone imprint

Tangled History is published by Capstone Press,
1710 Roe Crest Drive, North Mankato, Minnesota 56003
www.mycapstone.com

Library of Congress Cataloging-in-Publication data
Names: Otfinoski, Steven, author.
Title: The Great Chicago Fire : all is not lost / by Steven Otfinoski.
Description: North Mankato, Minnesota : Capstone Press, [2019]
Series: Tangled history | Includes bibliographical references and index.
Audience: Ages 8 to 14.
Identifiers: LCCN 2018012324 (print) | LCCN 2018015971 (ebook)
ISBN 9781515779667 (eBook PDF)
ISBN 9781515779315 (hardcover : alk. paper)
ISBN 9781515779629 (pbk. : alk. paper)
Subjects: LCSH: Great Fire, Chicago, Ill., 1871—Juvenile literature.
Fires—Illinois—Chicago—History—19th century—Juvenile literature.
Chicago (Ill.)—History—To 1875—Juvenile literature.
Classification: LCC F548.42 (ebook) | LCC F548.42 .084 2019 (print)
DDC 977.3/1103—dc23
LC record available at https://lccn.loc.gov/2018012324

Editorial Credits
Adrian Vigliano, editor; Bobbie Nuytten, designer; Jo Miller, media researcher; Kathy
McColley, production specialist

Photo Credits
Alamy: Chronicle, 55; Getty Images: Bettmann/Contributor, 93, Chicago History Museum/
Contributor, cover, 8, 11, 18, 43, 84, 96, 97, 99, Hulton Archive/Stringer, 6, MCT/Contributor,
105, Stock Montage/Contributor, 39; Library of Congress Prints and Photographs Division,
52, 56, 74, 79; Newscom: Glasshouse Images, 86, 90, KRT/Tribune File, 23, ZUMA Press/JT
Vintage, 32; North Wind Picture Archives, 16, 31, 67, 101; Science Source: 102; The Image
Works: ullstein bild/Gerstenberg, 46; Wikimedia: Library of Congress/W. Flint, 4, R.P.
Studley & Co., 72, Scan by NYPL/I. N. Phelps Stokes Collection of American Historical
Prints, 81, victorgrigas, 63

Printed in the Canada.
PA020

TABLE OF CONTENTS

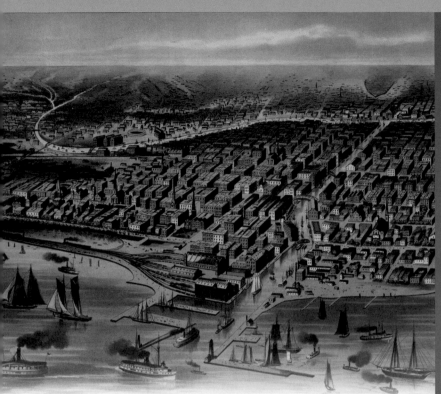

Chicago, Illinois, was a thriving American city in 1871.

FOREWORD

As the biggest city in the Midwest in 1871, Chicago was known as "The Gem of the Prairie." It was a bustling metropolis, a hub of commerce and business, and a center of modern technology for fighting fires.

Chicago had an up-to-date water system that featured a 15-story water tower, one of the city's tallest structures. The Chicago Fire Department had alarm call boxes throughout the city for citizens to call in fires. The department's horse-drawn steam engines could put out 600 gallons of water a minute.

All this technology was put to the test in the summer of 1871, one of the driest summers on record. The city received only 5 inches of rain between July and September. And fires occurred nearly every day. Chicago, like many American cities, was particularly vulnerable to fire. It was a city of wood—wooden buildings, wooden sidewalks, and even wooden streets. The dry wood was prime fuel for fire. And the fires didn't stop with the summer. In the first week of October alone there were 24 fires in the city.

Then on October 7 a huge fire broke out at the Lull and Holmes lumber mill west of downtown. It took more than 90 firefighters—half the department—15 hours to extinguish it. Some 20 acres were destroyed and estimates of the damage were in the vicinity of $1 million.

Chicago had become an important center for trade by 1871.

Sunday, October 8, dawned with weary firefighters still putting out the mill fire. The fire department was doing its best. But it needed more men and equipment to handle the constant flare-ups. However, the City Council didn't want to spend the money. Also local businesses were against stricter building codes that would lead to expensive new construction.

The people of Chicago went about their Sunday enjoying the weekend's simple pleasures. They rode bicycles in Lincoln Park and frolicked on the beaches along Lake Michigan. They enjoyed the unseasonably warm, summery weather. Their spirits weren't dampened by thoughts of more fires.

"THE BARN IS AFIRE!"

Fire Engine Company 21 was the first African American fire company in Chicago.

Robert Williams

Randolph Street, Chicago, Illinois,
October 8, 1871, 8:00 p.m.

Chicago Fire Marshal Robert Williams was being driven home after a long day. He closed his eyes, feeling the dry wind sweep across his face through the open wagon window.

"We are going to have a burn," he told the driver. "I can feel it in my bones."

The driver smiled and said nothing. Williams hoped in his heart that his bones were wrong this time. Fire had been a constant threat in the city for weeks. It was one of the worst fire seasons he could recall in his 23 years in the department. Things had not let up today. No sooner had they mopped up after the big fire at the mill than another one broke out. That one was a smaller fire on the South Side. Williams had supervised firefighters as they put out the fire and was now ready for a good night's sleep.

The wagon pulled up in front of his home on Randolph Street. Williams thanked the driver and climbed out. His wife was waiting for him at the door of their apartment building. Usually he would tell her all about his day, but he felt too tired to say more than a few words. He gave her a kiss on the cheek and headed straight for the bedroom.

Lying in the dark, Williams thought about the long day behind him. He wondered how many long days were to come before the temperatures fell, the winds calmed, and the fires died down. He prayed that they would get a break, if only for a few days. His men were exhausted and two of his steam engines were in the repair shop. It was clear that the wear and tear on equipment was beginning to take its toll. As he drifted off, Williams wondered if God had heard his prayer and would grant him one full night's sleep. He felt he had earned it.

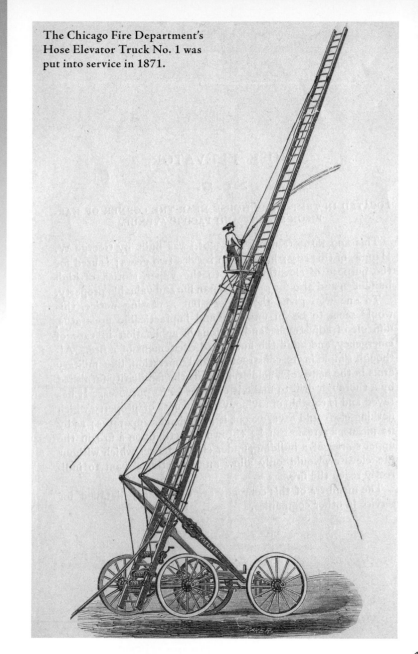

The Chicago Fire Department's Hose Elevator Truck No. 1 was put into service in 1871.

Cate O'Leary

137 De Koven Street, Chicago, Illinois, October 8, 1871, 8:15 p.m.

Cate O'Leary usually did not turn in so early, even on a Sunday night. But her sore foot had been acting up and a good night's rest seemed like the best medicine for it. She needed to be on her feet early the next morning to milk the five cows in the barn. After that she would take the wagon and deliver the milk to the neighbors on her route. Her husband, Patrick, would be off early to his job as a laborer. Between their jobs and the rent they took in from the tenant in the front rooms of their house they made a tidy living.

From her bed, O'Leary could hear singing and laughter from the other end of the house. Their tenant, Patrick McLaughlin, was throwing a party for his wife's brother who had just arrived in America from Ireland. She wished she felt well enough to join them.

McLaughlin was a good tenant who had a steady job with the railroad. Things had gone well for the O'Learys in the seven years since they had bought their shingled cottage. Life was good, O'Leary decided, as she closed her eyes and went to sleep.

Daniel "Peg Leg" Sullivan

De Koven Street, Chicago, Illinois, October 8, 1871, 8:35 p.m.

Dan Sullivan couldn't bring himself to go home. He had been visiting with the O'Learys, but then had to leave when they turned in for the night. The McLaughlins hadn't invited him in to their party. So he sat on the wooden boardwalk, tapping his wooden leg to the rhythm of the music they were making. The temperature had dropped just a bit and the October breeze, although dry, suited his spirits. But the morning would come soon enough and he'd be back at work driving a wagon. He heaved a sigh and rose to his feet.

It was then that he saw the flames. They were pouring out of the O'Learys' barn, only a hundred feet or so from where he stood. He began to shout, "Fire! Fire! Fire!" but heard no responses to his cries. The McLaughlins were making too much noise of their own to hear him and the O'Learys must have been sound asleep.

Sullivan decided he had to do something. He hobbled across the street to the barn and threw open the door. Smoke billowed out, choking him. But he rushed in and untied two of Cate O'Leary's cows. He saw another cow and a horse tied on the opposite wall and moved toward them. Before he could reach the wall, flames encircled him and he panicked and fell. His peg leg got caught in the floorboards. He began to crawl for the door when a calf bumped into him. He grabbed the rope around the calf's neck. Together, calf and man made their way out of the burning barn. Sullivan was burned but alive.

Cate O'Leary

137 De Koven Street, Chicago, Illinois, October 8, 1871, 8:45 p.m.

O'Leary awoke to the sound of her husband's voice. "Cate!" he cried, his eyes wide as saucers, "The barn is afire!"

She immediately thought of her cows and the horse. She leaped from the bed in her nightclothes and followed Patrick outside. The sight of the barn in flames was almost more than she could bear. A neighbor assured her that the animals had all gotten out, but her wagon was still inside. She tried to rush into the barn to pull it out, but Patrick stopped her. When she looked again, she could see it was too late to save the wagon. Together they joined their neighbors in a bucket brigade. They poured buckets of water on the house in an effort to save it from the same fate as the barn.

As she passed the buckets along, O'Leary didn't once look back at the conflagration that had consumed her barn.

People in the 1800s had to rely on bucket brigades as a first line of defense against fires.

Will Lee

133 De Koven Street, Chicago, Illinois,
October 8, 1871, 8:50 p.m.

Will Lee was about to leave for the South Side of Chicago with his brother-in-law and wife. Suddenly he heard his 17-month-old baby crying. He rushed back to the house, comforted the child, and opened the window. Looking out, he was stunned to see the O'Learys' barn burning brightly in the night. He could see in the flickering light of the flames a brigade pouring buckets of water on the O'Learys' house. He didn't go to help them. If the fire were to spread, buckets of water would not be enough to put it out. He decided he had to contact the fire department. Lee ran the three blocks to Bruno Gold's drugstore, where he knew there was a fire alarm.

"WHERE IS YOUR WATER, BILL?"

2

In 1871 the Chicago Fire Department was equipped with some of the best firefighting technology of the time.

Will Lee

Canal and Twelfth Street, Chicago, Illinois, October 8, 1871, 8:50 p.m.

Bruno Gold looked up from his counter as Will Lee rushed into the drugstore gasping for air.

"There's a fire on De Koven Street," he said. "I need the key to your alarm box."

"No need," he said. "The firefighters are already on their way. I heard an engine go by just minutes ago."

There was something smug about the druggist's response that Lee didn't like. But if what he said was true, it was a great relief.

Lee walked home. He could see that the fire had spread from the O'Learys' barn to other houses on De Koven. There was no fire engine in sight. Gold had been lying or mistaken, or the engine he heard had been going to another fire.

Lee cursed himself for not standing his ground and insisting on sending in the alarm. But he couldn't think of that now. He had to worry about his own home burning.

He got his wife and child out of the house at once. They retreated to a vacant lot to see where the fire would go next. Lee felt something soft rub up against him. He turned and saw the O'Leary's calf. The poor animal was only slightly burned by the fire. Lee petted the calf and it remained with him throughout the long night.

Robert Williams

Randolph Street, Chicago, Illinois, October 8, 1871, 9:00 p.m.

Williams was awakened from a sound sleep by a jab in his ribs. It was his wife's elbow. "Robert! FIRE!" she cried. He blinked his eyes and assumed that an alarm had been relayed to their apartment but hadn't awakened him.

Williams leaped from the bed. A fire wagon was already waiting outside to take him to the scene. He hoped it would not be as big a conflagration as the lumber mill fire had been.

His wagon pulled up on the south side of Taylor Street, where the fire had spread from De Koven. Here, two steam engines, the *America* and the *Chicago*, were already battling the flames with their water hoses.

"Hold on to her, boys!" Williams told the firefighters. Within minutes, a third engine, the *Illinois*, pulled up.

"Where is your water, Bill?" Williams asked the *Illinois'* pipe man, Bill Muller, who held the nozzle of the engine's water hose.

Muller and his men hauled out their heavy hose, with Williams pitching in. Muller aimed a steady stream of water at the flames. The heat from the fire was scorching and Muller quickly looked wilted.

"Marshal, I don't believe we can stand it here!" Muller said.

"Stand it as long as you can," Williams replied.

Then he turned to a nearby firefighter and told him to send out a second alarm for another engine and more men. The man headed for the nearest alarm—at Gold's drugstore.

Cate O'Leary

135 De Koven Street, Chicago, Illinois, October 8, 1871, 9:20 p.m.

Neighbors were working the bucket brigade, trying to save the O'Learys' home from the fire. So far it was safe, although other houses were ablaze. As O'Leary filled a bucket, she saw a firefighter approaching from an engine. She pointed him out to her husband.

"Can you soak down our place?" Patrick O'Leary asked the firefighter.

"What company carries your fire insurance?" the firefighter asked him.

Patrick grimaced. "We don't have no insurance," he replied.

Without a word, the firefighter moved on with his hose to the next house.

O'Leary wasn't surprised, just disgusted. She knew the firefighters only helped those residents with fire insurance.

Cate and Patrick O'Leary's house

"What kind of a city do we live in?" she asked her husband.

Patrick had no answer. Just then a second firefighter came by hauling a hose. O'Leary pleaded with him to wet down their house. He gave the walls a few splashes of water and then left.

"That's all the help we're getting," said Patrick. O'Leary nodded her head in agreement and went back to filling water buckets.

Eben Matthews

Peck Court, Chicago, Illinois, October 8, 1871, 9:25 p.m.

Eben Matthews was dead tired and ready for bed. A bookkeeper with the grain brokers Jones & Raymond, he had spent the previous night watching fires for entertainment. This was one of his favorite pastimes. He and his friend Andrew Dixon, who lived in the same boardinghouse, had gone out the previous night.

They had watched the lumberyard fire for hours. Now he needed a good night's sleep before the work week started.

But as he gazed out the boardinghouse window, Eben saw red and orange flames light up the night sky. "Dix," he said to his friend, "it's another fire. What do you say? Should we go?"

Dixon looked at the brightly lit sky and the same gleam came into his eye. "Sure, why not?" he replied. "We can always catch up on our sleep later."

They left the building, rushed up the street, and crossed the Polk Street Bridge. They reached the edge of the fire on the other side. A firefighter seemed to have the fire under control by now. Matthews was disappointed.

"Well, that's that," said Matthews with a sigh. "Let's go home."

They were almost at the bridge again when they heard a loud crackle and turned. The steeple of St. Paul's Roman Catholic Church was afire. Matthews assumed flying embers from the nearby burning buildings had ignited it.

"Looks like this fire still has some life left in it," Matthews said.

Dixon didn't seem to care. "I've seen enough fires for one weekend," he told his friend. "I'm heading back to bed."

Matthews knew he should go too, but he couldn't tear himself away. "I'll stick around for a while," he said. Dixon shrugged his shoulders and headed for the bridge. Then Matthews looked back at the church. It was soon enveloped in flames.

Bessie Bradwell

South Side, Chicago, Illinois,
October 8, 1871, 10:00 p.m.

Thirteen-year-old Bessie Bradwell was aroused from sleep by her mother.

"Wake up, dear. The city's on fire," her mother said. "We've got to leave the house as quickly as we can."

Bradwell knew her mother was not easily alarmed, and she spoke with a steadiness that was strangely comforting.

"Is our house going to burn down?" she asked.

"I don't know," replied her mother. "But we've got to get out in case it does. Now put on your clothes."

Bradwell got out of bed. She could hear her father, Judge James Bradwell, moving around with her brother. *They must be packing things to take with us,* she thought. Bradwell looked at her wardrobe and decided to wear her very best clothes in order to save them from the fire.

When she came downstairs her parents and brother were standing around a trunk that was filled with their things. "All right," said her father, closing the trunk, "let's get going."

"What about Polly?" Bradwell asked, pointing to their pet bird in its birdcage.

Father quickly agreed they should take the bird. Her brother picked up the birdcage and they went outside.

"You and the children head down Washington Street to Lincoln Park and the lake," her father told her mother. "You'll be safe there. Even if the fire should reach the park, you've got the water."

"But where are you going?" her mother asked.

"I'm going to my office," he explained. "I want to save those old law books I've been collecting for years. If there's anything worth saving from the flames it's them."

Bradwell wasn't surprised. She knew how much books meant to both her parents. After all, her mother was the founder and editor of the *Chicago Legal News*.

"Don't worry," her father continued. "I'll join you at the lake in a short time. Then we'll all be together."

For the first time her mother was showing signs of worry. "But how will you ever find us with all the people?" she asked.

"Don't worry," said her father. "I'll find you."

Her mother accepted this and reached for Bradwell's hand.

"I want to go with father," Bradwell said.

Neither parent argued with her. There wasn't time.

"All right," said her father. "We'll split up two and two." Then he took Bradwell's hand and together they watched her mother and brother disappear down the street, carrying the trunk.

Robert Williams

Randolph Street, Chicago, Illinois, October 8, 1871, 10:10 p.m.

Fire Marshal Williams oversaw his firefighters like a general on a battlefield. There were now five steam engines on the scene and three hose carts. But despite these resources and all his efforts, the enemy was winning.

Sweeping winds carried the fire over buildings and streets with frightening speed.

It only made a large fire that was already spreading that much harder to get under control. The greedy flames devoured every wooden building in their path. And now fire had spread beyond the land. The fierce heat ignited the layer of grease and oil that floated on the Chicago River along South Beach. It looked as if the very water was on fire.

At 10:30 p.m., Williams turned in the third alarm, calling out all 15 of Chicago's steam engines. He still had hope that an all-out effort could contain the fire and extinguish it.

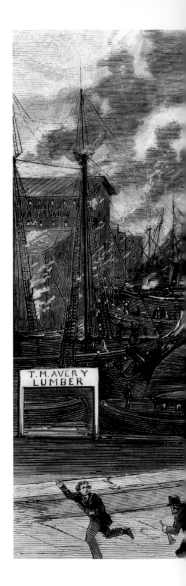

Strong winds carried fire onto and over the
Chicago River during the Great Fire.

"THIS IS THE END OF CHICAGO"

HARPER'S WEEKLY.
A JOURNAL OF CIVILIZATION

VOL. XV.—No. 774.]   NEW YORK, SATURDAY, OCTOBER 28, 1871.   [WITH A SUPPLEMENT. PRICE TEN CENTS.

Entered according to Act of Congress, in the Year 1871, by Harper & Brothers, in the Office of the Librarian of Congress, at Washington.

Harper's Weekly was one of the most popular magazines in the United States in the 1870s. The October 28, 1871, cover showed people who had been made homeless by the Chicago Fire.

John Chapin

Randolph Street, Chicago, Illinois,
October 8, 1871, 10:15 p.m.

John Chapin was enjoying a rare evening
of solitude. A leading illustrator for *Harper's
Weekly,* he was used to traveling from one
city and one story to another. He tried to
bring events to life with his drawings for the
magazine. He had arrived in Chicago earlier
that afternoon and checked into the six-story
Sherman House, one of Chicago's finest hotels.

With no immediate assignment on
his schedule, Chapin settled in early. He
was reading a book in bed when the fire
alarm sounded. He knew that Chicago was
experiencing a rash of fires and had no desire to
go chasing after this one. He ignored the alarm
and continued to read. At about 10:30 p.m. he
put down his book, extinguished the room's gas
light, and went to sleep.

It wasn't long before his sleep was disturbed by odd noises outside his room. First he heard a key rattling in his door lock. Then a bit later he heard heavy footsteps and loud voices coming from the hallway. And then there was this loud crackling noise outside the building. Unable to sleep, Chapin went to the window and lifted the blinds. What he saw made his blood run cold. A column of fire was shooting straight up into the sky. The entire street appeared to be in flames.

Chapin quickly dressed, packed his small suitcase, and left the room. The hallway was filled with fellow guests racing by with suitcases in hand or dragging trunks across the carpeted floor. Chapin went to retrieve his overcoat from the coat closet, but it was locked. Everyone, including the employees, was fleeing the hotel. Chapin pulled up the collar of his shirt and stepped out into the street. The night was surprisingly warm. Soon he joined the stream of bodies pushing its way along Randolph Street, away from the mounting flames.

Bessie Bradwell

Washington Street, Chicago, Illinois,
October 8, 1871, 11:00 p.m.

As Bradwell and her father reached his law office, he rushed inside and began pulling law books from the shelves. The books were heavy and her father insisted that Bradwell not try to lift them. A big man, he carried pile after pile of books down the stairs to the front entrance.

As she looked around the office, Bradwell found a way to be helpful. She discovered a book containing all the names and addresses of the subscribers to her mother's law journal. She knew this was valuable information that her mother would want saved from the fire. She carried it downstairs, even though it was nearly as hefty as one of her father's law books. Her father, red-faced and sweating, told Bradwell to wait for him inside. He was going to look for an express man who could load the books into his wagon.

Minutes passed. Five. Ten. Fifteen. Bradwell was afraid that something had happened to her father. Otherwise, why hadn't he returned? She stepped out into the street, leaving the book behind. The crowd of people had turned into an unruly mob, running for their lives in panic. Bradwell felt something hot on her head. She looked up and saw what looked like a snowstorm. The flakes falling from the sky were not white, however, but red. They were burning embers drifting on the wind from the fire. Hot air burned her lungs. Bradwell was about to step back into the building when she saw a pair of familiar faces pass by. It was a couple that were friends of her parents. They recognized her at once and asked what she was doing in the street alone. "My father . . ." she gasped. "I'm waiting for him. . . ."

"You can't stay here," said the man. "The fire is moving this way. You've got to leave at once."

The man went to grab her hand, but Bradwell turned and ran inside the building.

She lifted her mother's account book and returned. Clutching the book close, she gave the man one hand and they hurried down the street.

Robert Williams

Chicago, Illinois,
October 8, 1871, 11:15 p.m.

Williams could see that, despite all the department's efforts, the enemy was winning the battle. Unable to stand the scorching heat, firefighters were pulling back their engines from the front line. Some of them retreated so quickly that they dropped their hoses, leaving them to burn.

One of Williams' firefighters, Alex McMonagle, came running to him, a stretch of hose dangling from his shoulder. "Robert!" he cried. "The fire is on the South Side!"

"The devil it is!" replied Williams. "Go for it! I'll be there in a minute!"

The fire was spreading at a pace that stunned him. Williams tried unsuccessfully to move one stranded engine out of the fire's path with the help of volunteers. Then he leaped onto the *Washington*, a hose cart, and followed McMonagle to the South Side. He hoped he'd get there in time to save the city's gasworks from the fire.

He was too late. The gasworks were already in flames when he arrived. Disregarding the cries of his fellow firefighters, Williams rushed into the gasworks yard. He quickly saw there was nothing he could do to stem the tide of the fire. He rushed out from the yard and saw another blazing building just south of where he stood. It was the armory, which was being used as a temporary headquarters for the police. Suddenly the earth beneath his feet shook as the magazine in the armory exploded.

Williams proceeded a block north to Monroe Street. Here, the Merchants' Union Express Company barn was burning.

Fighting the Great Chicago Fire was
exhausting, dangerous work.

He urged on the steam engine crew to try to extinguish the flames. But, as Williams watched, the fire leaped over the firefighters and continued on its path of destruction.

Eben Matthews

Between Polk Street and Washington Boulevard, Chicago, Illinois, October 8, 1871, 11:20 p.m.

Matthews was moving down the street with the oncoming flood of people. He suddenly saw a man dragging a trunk with one hand while holding a child with his other hand. Without thinking, Matthews grabbed a handle on the trunk. He helped the man carry it to the corner of Polk and Wells streets. He then began running north.

It took Matthews several minutes to reach the Chamber of Commerce building at the corner of LaSalle and Washington. Here were the offices of his employers, Jones and Reynolds.

Matthews decided he would stop and help save whatever he could before the fire reached the building.

The offices were empty except for the building's janitor. Together, the two men went up to the roof. Sparks and firebrands carried along by the wind from burning buildings were raining down on the roof. Matthews grabbed a broom from the janitor and swept the sparks off the roof as they fell. He told the janitor to go downstairs and check on how far away the fire was. Then he went back to sweeping off the sparks.

John Chapin

The Washington Street Tunnel, Chicago, Illinois, October 8, 1871, 11:30 p.m.

As he crossed the tunnel, Chapin made himself useful. He helped an old lady carry her belongings. He held a baby for its mother while she attended to her six other children.

Drenched in sweat from his long walk, he ducked into a boardinghouse and put on clean clothes from his suitcase.

After leaving the boardinghouse he walked north to the Randolph Street Bridge. From here he had a panoramic view of the burning city. He could have kept going, but the view was extraordinary. It seemed he was the only person in Chicago at that moment to capture it. A true professional, Chapin found a comfortable spot to sit. He took out his drawing pad and a pencil and began to sketch the fire and the people fleeing from it.

John Chapin's illustration of people fleeing over the Randolph Street Bridge was later printed in *Harper's Weekly.*

Bessie Bradwell

Lake Street Bridge, Chicago, Illinois,
October 8, 1871, 11:30 p.m.

Bradwell followed the couple down Washington Street to Lake Street. They were in search of a bridge that wasn't on fire like others they'd passed. When they got there, however, the Lake Street Bridge, like so many other structures in the area, was on fire.

"Come on," urged the man. "The fire's not that bad yet. We can still get over the bridge if we hurry."

Bradwell hesitated and clutched her mother's subscription book more tightly to her chest. If she went with the couple she would be farther from the lake and her mother.

"Come, come with us," said the man impatiently, "we must get over the bridge at once."

Has my father already passed this way? Bradwell thought. *Is he alive and at the lake with my mother and brother?*

Just then a man, sweat running down his face, rushed by them, crying in a loud voice, "This is the end of Chicago!"

"No, no," replied Bradwell. "She will rise again."

Then she looked up at the smiling faces of the couple and took the man's hand. Together the three of them ran toward the bridge.

"TIME TO GET OUT"

4

Many parts of Chicago became dangerous as crowds
of people panicked and tried to get to safety.

Eben Matthews

Chamber of Commerce
Building, Chicago,
Illinois, October 8, 1871, 11:45 p.m.

Bright sparks and red embers rained down on him. Matthews decided there was no more he could do to save the roof and the building under it. He would see what he could salvage inside the offices of his employers.

Heading back inside, he ran into the janitor. "The fire. It's getting closer," the janitor said breathlessly. "Time to get out."

But Matthews was not getting out. Not just yet. He went to the office safe and opened it. He grabbed handfuls of papers and small accounting books and laid them on the wooden floor.

He knew that if the fire overtook the building, the small safe would not withstand the heat. He thought about the bank vault of the Northwestern National Bank office in the northwest corner of the building. That was one place where he knew the company papers would be safe.

He entered the bank's office, his arms filled with papers and books. The bank president, George Sturges, seemed to be making his own preparations to leave. He looked up and saw Matthews.

"Mr. Sturges," Matthews said, "can I move our company's papers and books to your vault?"

Sturges looked at a loss for words but quickly recovered. "I don't think that our vault is worth much, but you are welcome to put those books there if you wish," he said.

Matthews thanked him and Sturges opened the vault. Before Matthews had closed the vault, the bank president was gone. He looked around the office, as empty as his own.

Just then there was a rap at the window. Matthews looked out and saw a red-faced firefighter frowning at him.

"You've got to get out now!" the firefighter yelled through the windowpane.

His mission accomplished, Matthews did just that. In the street, he could see that the fire was closing in on this neighborhood. It was also spreading across the horizon to the city's North Side. Matthews wondered if anything in Chicago would be spared.

Robert Williams

Chicago, Illinois,
October 8, 1871, 11:50 p.m.

Williams made a futile search for more engines to fight the spreading fire. But he found only one, the *Illinois*, still battling the blaze. He had no sooner returned to the South Side when he got worse news. The fire had spread.

Buildings were now buring north across the river where the city's waterworks were located. He raced to the North Side and saw that the flames were consuming the waterworks. He was beginning to feel as if he were powerless to do anything to stop the fire. It was a feeling he'd never felt before and it came with shame and guilt. He headed for the South Side again. When he arrived, a firefighter told him that the fire was only 150 feet east of his home. Anxious to save his wife, along with what he could from inside the apartment, Williams rushed home.

When he arrived at his apartment he found a police captain and a few firefighters already there. They were helping his wife remove furniture from the apartment. With the help of another firefighter, Williams moved the family piano out into the street. Then he turned to go back through the door when he heard a terrible crash. The windowpanes had shattered from the heat.

Williams started back up the stairs. A wall of heat hit him. He could go no farther up the staircase. He turned and ran out the front door. He watched the flames eat away at his home and thought how he had failed to even save that. Unable to watch any longer, he turned to his weeping wife and gave her a hug. He told her he would return as soon as he could. Then he left to direct the few firefighters still in the battle. Most of the firefighters, finding no water left in the reserves, gave up the fight and went home.

Phil Sheridan

Michigan Avenue, Chicago, Illinois,
October 8, 1871, 11:55 p.m.

Phil Sheridan, one of the greatest Union generals of the Civil War, was a new resident of Chicago. He was dressed for bed when news of the fire reached him. Sheridan decided at once to investigate. He would see what he could do to stem the tide of flames.

Phil Sheridan

He quickly dressed and headed toward the military's division headquarters on the corner of LaSalle and Washington streets. In the street he worked his way through a mass of humanity. As he got closer to headquarters, the heat became so intense he had to abandon his attempt.

A resourceful soldier, Sheridan decided to set up a command post near the lakefront. So far, the shore of Lake Michigan was safe.

He sent word to soldiers stationed in the city to summon his staff. Sheridan didn't yet have a plan to stop the fire, but he knew that in time he would develop one. Having survived a bloody war, he believed he could survive, and triumph, over a fire.

James Bradwell

Lincoln Park, Chicago, Illinois,
October 9, 1871, 12:00 a.m.

The two hours since he'd left Bessie at his law offices had been nerve-wracking for Judge Bradwell. Unable to find someone to transport his law books to safety, he returned to the office to find Bessie gone.

He left the law books where they lay and started searching the streets for his daughter. Having no luck, he prayed that she had gone to the lake to find her mother and brother. Bradwell then headed for the lake, hoping to find his family.

As he walked, he passed piles of dry goods dumped on the lakeshore to be saved from the fire. Eventually he found his wife and son sitting in the park, their trunk lying nearby.

"Where is Bessie?" were the first words out of his mouth.

His wife stared at him. "Why, I thought she was with you," she replied.

Judge Bradwell sat heavily on the trunk and put his hands to his head. "Good god," he whispered hoarsely. "What has become of our girl?"

Mrs. Bradwell refused to give up hope. "I'd trust that girl to go to the ends of the earth—she'll come out all right, don't you worry."

Bradwell desperately wanted to believe that was true.

As the fire spread through Chicago, many streets
were blocked by fire or debris.

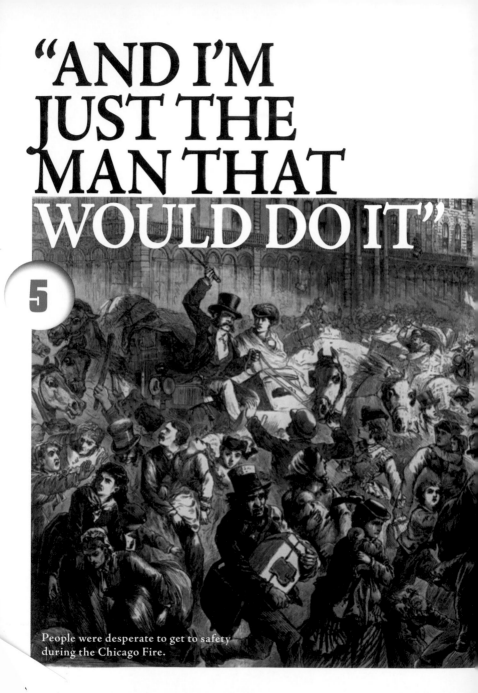

"AND I'M JUST THE MAN THAT WOULD DO IT"

5

People were desperate to get to safety during the Chicago Fire.

Mary Fales

Mary Fales was awakened by her husband, David.

"Look, Mary," he said, pointing to their bedroom window. "Fire. And it's headed this way."

Fales sat up in bed and saw the sky lit an unearthly orange. It struck her as beautiful, and then she realized what it meant.

"How far away is it, David?" she asked him. Surely he was wrong. Surely they would not have to leave the home they loved.

"I don't know. Three miles?" said David. "But with these strong winds it could be upon us quickly. We'd best pack what we can and leave."

The serious tone of his voice convinced her they could not stay. David was a lawyer and a very good one. She had trusted him from the day they married and she had to trust him now.

"You pack what you think is most valuable in the big trunk and I'll be back shortly," he said.

"Where are you going?" she said, fear creeping into her voice.

"The Wheeler boy has been good enough to let us use his horse," explained David. "Now I've got to see if I can get a buggy."

He didn't say where they would go with the buggy, but one place came into her mind—the Hutchinsons'. They lived north of Lincoln Park, a part of the city which the fire had not yet reached. Mrs. Hutchinson, whom everyone called "Aunt Eng," was one of Mary's dearest friends, a kind of second mother to her. Surely Aunt Eng and her husband would take them in le they waited out the fire.

David returned half an hour later with an open-top buggy that he hitched to the horse. Then he and Fales loaded the trunk and whatever else of their possessions they could fit into the buggy. They left just enough room for themselves. Fales told him where she thought they should go and he quickly agreed.

Then he snapped the reins and the horse began to run. The streets were swollen with people and animals, all running from the fire. Fales had never seen anything like it in her life. The going was slow, but they finally arrived at the Hutchinsons'. Aunt Eng came out to greet them. After seeing their pale faces and dirty clothes she seemed to need no further explanation of why they were there. "You must come in at once," she said.

"Mary's staying," said David, "but I'm going back to the house to get more of our things while there's still time."

Fales pleaded with him not to go, but he wouldn't listen.

"There is little danger, Mary," he insisted, "and I'll be back before the fire grows worse." With her arms around Aunt Eng, Fales watched David start back to West White Street with the empty buggy. Tears clouded her eyes. Despite his words, she wondered if she would ever see her dear husband again.

Eben Matthews

State Street, Chicago, Illinois, October 9, 1871, 2:15 a.m.

Having left the offices of Jones and Reynolds, Matthews was in a good mood. He had done what he could to help and could now go home with a satisfied mind. After he walked a while, he came upon his friend George Cole, a salesman for a carpet company. George was loading goods onto an express wagon and seemed happy to see Matthews.

"Where are you taking all those goods, George?" Matthews asked.

"Down to the lakefront," he replied. "It's the safest place left in the whole city from the fire. I hear thousands of people are down there. Businesses have dumped thousands of boxes and crates of their goods to save them from the fire."

"What can I do to help you?" Matthews asked.

"There's still a load of carpets inside to be taken to Mr. Hollister's house—he's my boss," said George. "If you could find another express wagon to take them there I'm sure Mr. Hollister would pay you back for whatever it costs."

Matthews said he would help. He stepped out into the street and tried to flag down an express wagon. Two or three whizzed by, one nearly striking him. Then one wagon stopped and the driver agreed to take the carpets to Hollister's home on Wabash Avenue for $25. Matthews paid him the money, hoping that George was right and that he'd get it back. Then he returned to help George finish his packing.

James Bradwell

Judge Bradwell tried to put thoughts of Bessie out of his mind. If his wife had faith in Bessie's survival skills, then he would try to as well. Lincoln Park, adjacent to the lake, was filled with a seemingly endless sea of humanity. Families, single men, groups of women, and homeless people were all crowded together. People were surrounded by their belongings, which consisted of a multitude of sizes of trunks, boxes, and furniture. They all saw the park and lakefront as a refuge from the fire that was devouring the city. Many seemed to believe that the flames would not reach them here.

But Bradwell was not so optimistic. He had felt the power of the fire up close at his office on Washington Street. He had seen the flames and firebrands leap a river and felt the lake, while safer, was still vulnerable to the intense heat.

To many people fleeing the Great Chicago Fire, Lincoln Park seemed to be a safe destination.

And even if the park remained a haven from the fire, it left people and their possessions at the mercy of thieves.

Bradwell had already seen groups of criminals plundering trunks and was determined they would not get into his. He told his wife and son he'd be back soon and went to a nearby friend's house and borrowed a shovel. Then he returned to the park and began to dig a hole in which to put the trunk.

The buried trunk would remain safe from fire and thieves and he could come back and dig it up later.

A police officer came by and ordered Bradwell to stop digging. "Sir," said the officer in a heavy voice, "you are defacing the ball grounds."

Ball grounds! thought Bradwell. *The city is on fire and this officer is worried about the playing fields for amateur ball players?* All the anger and frustration inside him rose up in his throat. He raised the shovel in his trembling hands and the officer stepped back in alarm.

"You go on," said Bradwell, "or I'll make you see more stars than you ever saw in your life!"

Mrs. Bradwell, who had been watching this drama, let out a gasp. The judge may well have gasped too at his own rash words, expecting the police officer to arrest him. But the officer looked up at the 6-foot-4-inch tall man and said, "Oh, go on, Captain. Go on." With that he moved away.

"I'm not a captain!" cried Bradwell. "I'm a judge!"

But by then the officer was out of earshot.

Richard Bellinger

Lincoln Place, Chicago, Illinois,
October 9, 1871, 7:00 a.m.

Chicago police officer Richard Bellinger loved his home. He had built it with his own hands and presented it as a gift to his new bride. It was where he wanted to raise his family and grow old. This was why when Bellinger heard the news of the approaching fire he decided he had to do something. Unlike many Chicagoans, he would not abandon his house to the flames— not without a fight. Because his home was in the north end of the city, he had time to prepare. He summoned his brother-in-law, another police officer, to help. He knew that saving his home was a job that needed two pairs of hands.

First they raked up all the leaves around the house. Bellinger knew that the leaves would easily catch fire and spread it. Then they went to work tearing up the wooden sidewalk, picket fence, and steps in front of the house.

65

The goal was to create a barrier against the flames. They carried the torn wood to a nearby vacant lot and burned it. Next they fetched buckets of water from a nearby well and soaked rugs and blankets. They carried the wet materials up to the shingle roof. Bellinger hoped this would protect the roof from the burning cinders that would soon be falling.

As Bellinger carried another blanket to the well, he ran into his brother-in-law, who was shaking his head.

"What's wrong?" he asked.

"It's the well, Richard," his brother-in-law said. "It's run dry."

Bellinger dropped the blanket. He could not have gotten worse news at such a moment. He rubbed his brow and started to think.

James Bradwell

Lincoln Park, Chicago, Illinois,
October 9, 1871, 7:30 a.m.

Judge Bradwell's prediction had come true.
The fire now encircled the park, driving people
closer and closer to the lake. The endless stacks
of goods and possessions began to catch fire.

Once in Lincoln Park, people tried
to set up their camps as close to
Lake Michigan as possible.

And the heat and wind only seemed to grow stronger. Burning mattresses gave off a noxious smell that made Mrs. Bradwell gag. The judge gave her a handkerchief to hold over her face.

People were running into the lake now, standing up to their waists in the chilly waters to escape the intense heat.

"Come on," Bradwell said to his wife and son. They followed him down to the edge of the lake. Then they entered the murky waters, but only so far that the water came up to the adults' shins. The judge felt that was far enough to preserve their dignity. He felt that maintaining their dignity was important, even in a time of disaster. All three bent down and splashed water on their faces and arms. Gazing up at the encircling flames, Bradwell wondered how long they would have to endure this ordeal.

Phil Sheridan

Downtown, Chicago, Illinois,
October 9, 1871, 10:00 a.m.

General Sheridan had his plan. He would blow up every building on Harrison Street, an avenue that cut straight across the city. When the fire reached Harrison, it would have nowhere to go and it would burn itself out. Firefighters called this a firebreak.

The soldiers followed Sheridan's orders and blew up building after building until they ran out of dynamite. The general traveled to a building on Michigan Avenue where the city's gunpowder was kept. He intended to use it to continue the demolition of buildings. When he arrived there he found a watchman on duty.

"I need the gunpowder to fight the fire," he told the man.

The man did not seem to recognize Sheridan and appeared unimpressed. He refused to let Sheridan take the gunpowder.

"What's your name?" Sheridan asked sternly.

"Mahoney," replied the watchman. "Do you want me to spell it for you?"

Furious, Sheridan turned on his heels and left. He found a man who had some authority in the city and returned to the building with him. Again the watchman said he was not convinced of their mission and he would not turn over the gunpowder. Finally, Sheridan found a police officer and led him back to the building.

"If this man doesn't give us the gunpowder, I want you to arrest him," Sheridan told the officer.

Mahoney pulled a revolver from his pocket.

"If you get any gunpowder, it will only be after this revolver is empty," he vowed, "and I'm just the man that would do it."

Sheridan gave up the fight and sent for more artillery to continue his mission. Then he engaged soldiers to tear down another house while he himself took an ax to one corner of the same house.

As Sheridan swung his ax, he sensed that the fire's progress was slowing. After all his troubles, the firebreak seemed to be working. He had won the battle to save Harrison Street. But the outcome of the larger war was still very much in question.

Mary Fales

North of Lincoln Park, Chicago, Illinois, October 9, 1871, 10:15 a.m.

Fales was not the only refugee to find her way to Aunt Eng's. The house was crowded with people. One lady had arrived with four servants. Another, having just been married, brought her wedding presents with her. The men in their families were mostly gone, trying to salvage their belongings like David Fales. The women tried to make small talk but the fire dominated every conversation.

David returned at noon. He told Fales he had gotten nearly everything out of their house.

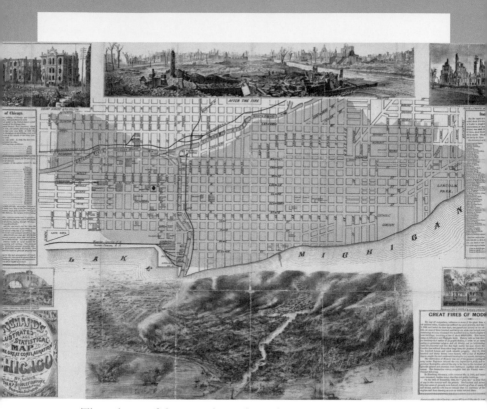

The red area of this map shows the path
of the Great Fire through Chicago.

He said he had buried their piano, books,
and her china dishes in a neighbor's yard.
All was safe.

"And what about the house?" Fales
asked him.

"Burnt to the ground," he said, "along
with most of the street. I'm sorry, Mary."

She held him close and tried to hold back her tears. She loved that house but it wasn't as important as their lives. They still had each other and for that she was grateful.

"WE MAY GO THROUGH IN SAFETY OR WE MAY DIE IN THE ATTEMPT"

6

Chicago's air filled with smoke as the fire burned.

Richard Bellinger

Lincoln Place, Chicago, Illinois,
October 9, 1871, 10:20 a.m.

Richard Bellinger knew where he could find more water. Ten-Mile Ditch was a water hole just one block east of Hudson Avenue. Bellinger and his brother-in-law went there and filled buckets and carried them back. They climbed a ladder to the roof and continued to pour water on the steaming shingles. Most of the roof was safe, but there were still a few spots smoldering from fallen embers.

"Should we go back to the ditch for more water?" asked Bellinger's brother-in-law.

"No," said Bellinger. "I have something in the cellar that will finish the job."

He led the way down to the cellar and pointed to a keg of cider.

"You're going to waste good cider on a fire?" asked the other man.

Bellinger grinned. "I can always get more cider, but I only have one house," he replied. "Come on, give me a hand with this keg."

James Bradwell

Lincoln Park, Chicago, Illinois,
October 9, 1871, 10:45 a.m.

It had been a long night and morning for the Bradwells and thousands of other Chicagoans at Lincoln Park. But now the fire seemed spent, at least in the park. Weary and shivering, people emerged from the lake to see what, if anything, was left of their valuables.

Judge Bradwell was grateful that he had thought to bury his treasure. Now he left the water and was pleased to discover that his shovel had escaped the flames.

He went to the spot where he had buried the trunk and began to dig. In a short time he reached the trunk and pulled it up onto the burnt grass.

A group of express men and their wagons, looking for work, were not far away. Bradwell grabbed one of them. "Will you take us down to Michigan Avenue for $50?" he asked the man.

"I will," said the express man. He pulled his wagon to the trunk and loaded it on board. Then he looked up at the rising smoke coming from the direction they would be traveling. Apparently changing his mind, he pulled the trunk off the wagon.

Judge Bradwell felt his face get hot and he glared at the man. "Take your choice of three things: take us as you agreed to and we may go through in safety or we may die in the attempt, or you may stay right here and die now."

The express man made the right decision and lifted the trunk back on his wagon. The three Bradwells then climbed aboard. Mrs. Bradwell looked worried at the poor bird in its cage that sat in her lap. It was gasping for air.

"Don't worry," said her husband. "He'll make it. We're all going to make it." But even as he said this, his thoughts turned again to his missing daughter.

Robert Williams

Chicago Avenue, Chicago, Illinois,
October 9, 1871, 11:00 a.m.

Williams' eyes were so swollen by the smoke and heat that he could barely see. The entire west end of Chicago Avenue was ablaze. Worse still, there were no firefighters left to even make an attempt to halt the flames. But Williams wasn't quitting. He took a wagon to the West Side, the one part of the city still unscathed by the fire. He had to get a pair of goggles to protect his eyes.

Williams saw engines arriving from other cities, answering the call of Mayor Roswell Mason. One came from as far away as Milwaukee, Wisconsin, a distance of more than 90 miles. But these new engines did not raise Williams' spirits.

He knew they were too late to make much of a difference now. With sweat-drenched clothes and aching eyes, Williams drove to the nearby refuge where his wife was staying.

In many parts of Chicago, the Great Fire continued burning all the way to the shore of Lake Michigan.

Williams found his wife, hugged her, and then changed clothes. After that, he drank a cup of tea and tried to swallow two mouthfuls of bread, but couldn't. Finally he said goodbye to his wife and headed back to the fire.

Mary Fales

North of Lincoln Park,
Chicago, Illinois,
October 9, 1871, 5:00 p.m.

All afternoon Fales, her husband, David, and the others at Aunt Eng's watched the people passing by. They were on their way farther north away from the fire. Some rode in wagons filled with their belongings. Others carried bags or dragged trunks along the street. It made Fales think of the Bible story in which the Israelites fled Egypt, pursued by the pharaoh's army.

One by one, the people around them in Aunt Eng's house gathered their things and left. The fire was approaching even this safe haven. David and the other men helped bury belongings, including Aunt Eng's, outside on the grounds. Finally it was time for them all to leave. Fales found herself comforting Aunt Eng, the very woman who earlier had comforted her.

On the West Side of Chicago, people could see the East Side of the city being destroyed by towering flames just across the river.

Aunt Eng grew panicky. She claimed she had to find a shawl that someone left at her house long before the fire. David had found an old cart and filled it with their belongings, along with a trunk of Aunt Eng's. Aunt Eng herself left the house in the company of other friends.

The Faleses headed for the safety of the West Side. The problem was that most of the bridges on the way there had been destroyed by the fire. But David knew of at least one bridge that had still been intact when he last saw it.

David urged the horses on, but they were tired and irritable. They began to kick at the wagon, which was already in fragile condition. David snapped the reins and the horses stopped their kicking and plunged ahead. Mary held on tightly to the wooden seat.

They reached the bridge and found it still intact. Their wagon rumbled across it. From there they continued west, hoping to reach the home of a friend, Judge Parker.

Phil Sheridan

Michigan Avenue, Chicago, Illinois,
October 9, 1871, 9:00 p.m.

It had been a long day and General Sheridan was glad it was over. Unlike many Chicagoans, he was fortunate enough to still have a house to come home to. The fire had spared it, but his favorite horse, Breckinridge, had perished in the flames. He had also lost all his personal and professional papers. They had been housed in a War Department building that was destroyed in the fire.

The fire had nearly died, but not from his efforts or those of the fire department. Instead, Mother Nature had intervened. Rain had just started to fall across the city. The general felt it would put out what was left of the slowly dying fire. He was thinking about turning in for the night when there was a loud rapping on the front door.

PROCLAMATION

WHEREAS, In the Providence of God, to whose will we humbly submit, a terrible calamity has befallen our city, which demands of us our best efforts for the preservation of order and the relief of the suffering, be it known that the faith and credit of the City of Chicago is hereby pledged for the necessary expenses for the relief of the suffering.

Public order will be preserved. The police and special police now being appointed will be responsible for the maintainance of the peace, and the protection of property.

All officers and men of the Fire Department and Health Department will act as Special Policemen without further notice.

The Mayor and Comptroller will give vouchers for all supplies furnished by the different Relief Committees.

The headquarters of the City Goverament will be at the Congregational Church, corner of West Washington and Ann streets.

All persons are warned against any act tending to endanger property. Persons caught in any depredation will be immediately arrested.

With the help of God, order and peace and private property shall be preserved.

The City Government and the committees of citizens pledge themselves to the community to protect them, and prepare the way for a restoration of public and private welfare.

It is believed the fire has spent its force and all will soon be well.

R. B. MASON, Mayor.

GEO. TAYLOR, Comptroller. (By R. B. Mason.)
CHAS. C. P. HOLDEN, President Common Council.
T. B. BROWN, President Board of Police.

Mayor Roswell Mason issued several proclamations following the Great Fire in hopes of reestablishing law and order in Chicago.

He opened the door to see a small crowd of people. It was a delegation of citizens, led by city prosecutor Thomas W. Grosvenor.

"General," Grosvenor explained, "the worst of the fire is over, but the city is in chaos. There is mass looting in the streets and the mayor fears it will only get worse. He authorized me to come here and ask you to put Chicago under martial law."

Sheridan saw that the city needed him now more than ever. "I accept your offer," he told Grosvenor.

"ALL IS NOT LOST"

7

Areas of Chicago such as Wabash Avenue lay in ruins after the Great Fire.

Mary Fales

Two and a half hours west of
Aunt Eng's,
Illinois, October 10, 1871, 6:00 a.m.

The Faleses had arrived at Judge Parker's house in the early evening hours of October 9. They had spent a restless night in a guest bedroom. Too much had happened in the past 24 hours to allow Fales to sleep. She got up quietly so as not to disturb her husband and went to a desk in the room. Sitting down, she took out a piece of paper and pen and began to write a letter to her mother.

"Dear Mama," she began. "You have probably heard of our fire and will be glad to know that we are safe and sound after much trouble." Listening to the rainfall, she continued to write.

James Bradwell

Near Lincoln Park, Chicago, Illinois,
October 10, 1871, 8:00 a.m.

Like many people, the Bradwells had no home
to which to return, but that hardly concerned the
judge now. He left his wife and son at a safe place
in the park and went off in search of Bessie.

The city was a grim landscape of ruins. Whole
streets of buildings were razed to the ground
by the fire. Other streets were lined with the
smoldering ruins of buildings and homes. Rubble
and refuse were everywhere. People passed the
judge in a daze, acknowledging him and one
another with no more than a questioning stare.
The more he saw, the more Bradwell despaired.
What chance did he have of finding his little girl
in this sea of broken humanity? He sat down on
a piece of rubble and felt hot tears sting his eyes.
None of the people passing seemed to notice the
grown man crying. Each of them was preoccupied
with his or her own tale of woe.

General Sheridan was at last in his element. Yesterday's work had been frustrating and his efforts had brought little success. But now he was certain he could make a difference.

With the support of the secretary of war in Washington, Sheridan had gone to work. He had summoned rations, tents, and blankets from military stores in Missouri and Indiana. These goods would be distributed to the 30,000 homeless people now camped out in Lincoln Park.

Sheridan had also called out six regimental units from Kansas and Nebraska to come help. In addition to this, he planned to call on thousands of local civilians. He knew many people would be needed to help establish order and peace in the crippled city. He decided he'd call them Sheridan's Guards, to instill in them a sense of pride and community.

He was beginning to feel like his old self again. The worst was over, but people's suffering continued and he was going to help them the best he could.

Many people lost their homes during the Great Fire and continued to camp in the city as refugees.

Richard Bellinger

Lincoln Place, Chicago, Illinois,
October 10, 1871, 12:00 p.m.

Bellinger looked out at the city. Nearly every house in view had burned, but not his. His efforts had saved his home.

Bellinger shared his house with about 20 less fortunate neighbors. They had all lost their homes. He was thoughtful to his unexpected guests and did what he could to make them comfortable. Of course, when they were thirsty he could only offer them water. His cider keg, he explained, was empty, but for a good cause.

James Bradwell

Downtown, Chicago, Illinois,
October 10, 1871, 8:00 p.m.

Judge Bradwell didn't want to go to the citizens' meeting, but his wife insisted. It would take his mind off Bessie, she said. They had not found their daughter but still held out hope she was alive. Bradwell was thankful for his wife, and for her optimism and confidence. He didn't know what he would do without her.

The judge arrived a half hour late to the citizens' meeting. As he entered and sat, several men were asking the group if anyone had seen their wives, children, or siblings. Bradwell decided he would do the same and rose to his feet. "Has anyone here seen my daughter, Bessie?" he asked in a loud voice. "She is 13 years old and—"

Before he could say another word, a man jumped up from his chair. The judge recognized him as a neighbor and friend.

"Don't worry, Judge Bradwell," said the man, "your daughter is safe on the west side and she carted that great heavy *Legal News* subscription book for nine hours."

The judge rushed forward and embraced his friend as the crowd applauded. It was a miracle.

Some fire refugees had to rely on charities for items such as clothing.

Phil Sheridan

Michigan Avenue, Chicago, Illinois,
October 12, 1871, 11:30 a.m.

The last 48 hours had been very busy for
General Sheridan. He had spent much of his
time organizing the civilians who made up his
Sheridan's Guards. With their help, he had been
doing everything he could to see to the needs of
the people of Chicago. Now he sat down at his
desk and began writing a note to Mayor Roswell
Mason.

Dear Mayor Mason,

*No cause of outbreak or disorder has been
reported . . . and the people of the city are calm, quiet
and well-disposed.*

Sincerely yours,

General Philip Sheridan

Bessie Bradwell

Chicago, Illinois,
October 12, 1871, 1:00 p.m.

Bradwell was quarreling with her brother in the parlor of their new home when her parents entered the room.

"Well, I'm glad to see life has returned to normal for you children," said Mrs. Bradwell with a smile.

"I know we shouldn't fight," said Bessie, feeling a bit guilty. "Not when we have so much to be thankful for."

"That's true," said Mrs. Bradwell, hugging her daughter. "But I want you to remember something next time there is a fire. If your father and I separate, you are to stay with me!"

"We won't have another fire," said Bessie's brother. "If we do I'm moving to Philadelphia or New York."

"Quiet!" said their father, who was holding up the latest edition of the *Chicago Tribune*.

"I want you all to listen to this editorial in the paper." He cleared his throat. "All is not lost," he read. "Though four hundred million dollars' worth of property has been destroyed, Chicago still exists . . . the great arteries of trade and commerce all remain unimpaired . . . and all ready for immediate resumption . . ."

Chicago's First National Bank before the Great Fire

The judge put down the paper and turned to his family. "You mark my words," he said. "Chicago is going to be a bigger and better city than it ever was before that fire."

And Bessie believed every word her father said.

Chicago's First National Bank was almost destroyed in the fire.

EPILOGUE

The Great Chicago Fire was one of the worst natural disasters ever visited upon a major American city. More than 17,000 structures, including homes, businesses, and public buildings were destroyed with an estimated $200 million in damages. About 300 people perished in the fire, although only about 120 bodies were recovered. Some 100,000 people were left homeless. Fortunately, the stockyards, one of the busiest enterprises in the city, were spared. The railroad lines were also left intact. The functioning rail lines made it easier to begin rebuilding, a process that started almost immediately after the disaster.

A month after the fire, Joseph Medill was elected the new mayor of Chicago. He promised to create stricter building and fire codes to prevent another such disaster.

The Chicago Water Tower (bottom center) was the only public building in the fire's path to survive. It still stands today.

With so much of the city destroyed, architects were able to reconstruct the city from the ground up. They created sturdy, modern buildings, including the world's first skyscrapers. The city's economy boomed in this new setting. At the time of the fire, Chicago's population was 324,000. By 1880 it had grown to 500,000, and a decade later it was over a million. The Columbian Exposition, a world's fair, was held in Chicago in 1893. By then Chicago was one of America's greatest cities. It remains so today.

The end of the fire was only the beginning of a lifetime of troubles for Catherine and Patrick O'Leary. Their house, oddly enough, survived the massive fire. An official inquiry fixed no blame on the O'Learys for starting the fire. But a story of Catherine's cow kicking over a lantern and setting the barn ablaze spread quickly. The story, probably invented by an imaginative reporter, took on a life of its own. Soon the legend was accepted as fact. Today the story of the O'Learys' cow is the only thing many Americans know about the Chicago Fire.

By the 1890s Chicago
was a busy, thriving city
once again.

Catherine O'Leary denied she or her cow had caused the fire. But criticism grew so strong that the couple spent much of the rest of their lives hiding from public view. When a reporter asked Catherine if the fire had been pretty rough on her she responded, "Rough! Why, my God, man, it was a terror to the world!" She died in obscurity in 1895.

In 1997 the Chicago City Council passed a resolution. It officially exonerated Catherine O'Leary of any responsibility for the fire.

The story of Cate O'Leary and her cow became one of the most well-known myths of the Chicago Fire.

Today the Chicago Fire Department training academy is located on the site of the O'Leary property.

Daniel "Peg Leg" Sullivan, the first person to see the fire, testified at the inquiry and then disappeared. He probably left Chicago soon after. Some historians believe he may have accidentally started the fire, which would explain his appearance at the scene. Others say a passerby who carelessly tossed a match into the barn may have started the fire. Still others claim an anarchist group that wanted to burn down the city started it. One minister from Cincinnati, Ohio, claimed the fire was God's vengeance for Chicago allowing saloons to be open on Sundays!

Fire Marshal Robert Williams continued to serve his city faithfully. Judge James Bradwell was elected to the Illinois House of Representatives in 1873 and served two terms. He was a firm supporter of women's rights and in 1875 represented President Lincoln's widow, Mary Todd Lincoln. Her son Robert had placed her in a psychiatric hospital.

Bradwell's eloquence in the defense of Mary Todd Lincoln led the court to declare her competent to handle her own finances. The judge's wife, Myra, died in 1894. After her death he took over the publishing of *Chicago Legal News*, which she had founded in 1868. Bessie Bradwell served as her father's assistant on the journal. Judge Bradwell died in 1907.

Many Chicagoans hailed General Phil Sheridan as the hero of the Great Fire. He succeeded another Civil War general, William T. Sherman, as commander in chief of the U.S. Army in 1883. Sheridan died five years later in 1888. A statue of Sheridan was dedicated in 1924. It still stands today.

John Chapin's story about the fire and two of his illustrations appeared in *Harper's Weekly* soon after the fire. He continued to work for the magazine for many years and died in 1907.

Little is known of the post-fire lives of Will Lee, Eben Matthews, Mary Fales, and Richard Bellinger. However, both Matthews' and Fales' accounts of the fire were later published.

The story of Bellinger splashing a keg of cider on his house may be a myth, but his home still stands. It is one of the few houses in the area to survive the fire and has been lived in ever since. In 2005 it sold for $1.2 million.

The Bellinger house still stands in Chicago today.

TIMELINE

OCTOBER 8, 1871

8:35 P.M. Daniel "Peg Leg" Sullivan is the first person to see the fire in the O'Learys' barn on De Koven Street

8:45 P.M. The O'Learys and their neighbors try unsuccessfully to contain the fire

8:50 P.M. Neighbor Will Lee goes to send a fire alarm at a nearby drugstore but is discouraged by the store's owner

9:00 P.M. Fire Marshal Robert Williams rushes to the scene of the fire, now being combated by firefighters with several steam engines

10:00 P.M. The Bradwells, along with thousands of other Chicagoans on the South Side, flee their home and head for the safety of Lincoln Park, adjacent to Lake Michigan's shore

11:20 P.M. Eben Matthews is just one of many loyal employees who risk their lives going to their workplaces to save whatever can be salvaged before the fire sweeps through the buildings

11:30 P.M. John Chapin, illustrator for *Harper's Weekly*, draws some of the first sketches of the fire and its victims from the Randolph Street Bridge

11:50 P.M. Unable to stop the fire from spreading across much of the city, Fire Marshal Williams goes to his own home to save what he can before the fire reaches it

OCTOBER 9

12:00 A.M. General Phil Sheridan sets out to halt the fire by creating a firebreak with explosives

12:00 A.M. Judge James Bradwell joins his family and thousands of others in Lincoln Park near the lakeshore

7:00 A.M. Police officer Richard Bellinger works to save his Lincoln Place home from the fire

7:30 A.M. The refugees in Lincoln Park, alarmed by the approaching flames, wade into Lake Michigan to escape the fire and intense heat

11:00 A.M. Firefighters from other cities continue to arrive in Chicago, but the battle against the fire by now is essentially lost

5:00 P.M. The Fales and other Chicagoans flee west to the one section of the city still untouched by the fire

8:00 P.M. Rain falls on the city through the night, putting out what is left of the fire

9:00 P.M. A citizens' delegation visits General Sheridan and asks him to put Chicago under martial law

OCTOBER 10

10:00 A.M. General Sheridan, now in command, begins to summon and distribute supplies for the thousands of homeless people seeking refuge in Lincoln Park

8:00 P.M. At a citizens' meeting, Judge Bradwell receives word that his missing daughter, Bessie, has survived the fire

OCTOBER 12

11:30 A.M. General Sherman sends a note to Mayor Roswell Mason that martial law has made the city safe. The rebuilding of the city is already underway

GLOSSARY

anarchist (AN-ahr-kist)—a person who believes in a social system that calls for ending government and having people solve their problems as a group without elected leadership

armory (AR-muh-ree)—a place where weapons are stored

broker (BRO-kuhr)—a person who buys and sells stocks and bonds

bucket brigade (BUHK-it bri-GAYD)—a line of people formed to put out a fire by passing along buckets of water

buggy (BUH-gee)—a four-wheeled horse-drawn carriage

chaos (KAY-os)—total confusion

conflagration (kon-fluh-GRAY-shuhn)—a vast, destructive fire

editorial (ed-ih-TOR-ee-uhl)—a statement that expresses an opinion in a newspaper or magazine or on the radio or television

ember (EM-buhr)—the hot, glowing remainder of a fire

exonerated (ig-ZON-uh-rate-ehd)—cleared from blame or guilt

express man (ek-SPRESS MAN)—a worker who, before automobiles, transported goods by horse-drawn wagon from one place to another

firebrand (FYR-brand)—a burning piece of wood

insurance (in-SHU-ruhnss)—protection against loss or damage

magazine (MAG-uh-zeen)—a room where ammunition and explosives are stored

ration (RASH-uhn)—an amount of food or supplies allowed by a government

CRITICAL THINKING QUESTIONS

1. The Great Chicago Fire may not have been prevented, but it could have been far less deadly. Review the text and find three reasons why the fire spread so quickly out of control. What actions, if any, could have led to the fire being extinguished sooner?

2. By an amazing coincidence, the same night the Great Chicago Fire began an equally destructive fire swept across northern Wisconsin and into upper Michigan. The Great Peshtigo Fire destroyed more than a million acres of forest and took the lives of 1,200 people, four times the number who died in the Chicago Fire. It was the worst fire in U.S. history, but at the time Chicago got all the attention and continues to today. Why do you think this is so? Use other texts or valid Internet sources to research this question.

3. The city of Chicago arose from the ashes of the Great Fire a safer and greater U.S. metropolis. Research the years right after the fire and find out what the people of Chicago did to bring this about.

INTERNET SITES

Use FactHound to find Internet sites related to this book.

Visit *www.facthound.com*

Just type in 9781515779315 and go.

FURTHER READING

Bartoletti, Susan Campbell. *Down the Rabbit Hole: The Diary of Pringle Rose*. New York: Scholastic, 2013.

Cooper, Michael L. *Fighting Fire! Ten of the Deadliest Fires in American History and How We Fought Them*. New York: Henry Holt & Company, 2014.

Pascal, Janet B. *What Was the Great Chicago Fire?* New York: Grosset & Dunlap, 2016.

Tarshis, Lauren. *I Survived the Great Chicago Fire, 1871*. New York: Scholastic, 2015.

SELECTED BIBLIOGRAPHY

Angle, Paul M., ed. *The Great Chicago Fire: Described in Several Letters.* Chicago: Chicago Historical Society, 1946.

Burr, Frank A., and Richard J. Hinton. *The Life of General Philip H. Sheridan.* Providence, RI: J.A. and R.A Reid, 1888.

Cromie, Robert. *The Great Chicago Fire.* New York: McGraw-Hill, 1958.

The Great Chicago Fire and The Web of Memory. https://www.greatchicagofire.org/ Accessed June 1, 2017.

Kogan, Herman, and Robert Cromie. *The Great Fire: Chicago, 1871.* New York: G.P. Putnam's Sons, 1971.

Morris, H. Roy. *Sheridan: The Life and Wars of General Phil Sheridan.* New York: Crown Publishers, 1992.

"The Time Machine: Two Fires." *American Heritage* (October 1996): 118–119.

Wallenchinsky, David, and Irving Wallace. *The People's Almanac.* "Man-Made Disasters," pp. 555–556. Garden City, NY: Doubleday & Co., 1975.

INDEX

ABOUT THE AUTHOR

Steven Otfinoski has written more than 190 books for young readers. His previous books in the Tangled History series include *Day of Infamy: The Story of the Attack on Pearl Harbor*, *Tragedy in Dallas: The Story of the Assassination of John F. Kennedy*, and *Smooth Sea and a Fighting Chance: The Story of the Sinking of Titanic*. Among his many other books for Capstone is the Fact Finders book *The Triangle Shirtwaist Factory Fire*. Three of his nonfiction books have been named Books for the Teen Age by the New York Public Library. He lives in Connecticut with his wife and dog.